EVERY MANAGER'S GUIDE TO BETTER

EXIT
INTERVIEWING

FACE to FACE:
BLR Guides to Better Interviewing

EVERY MANAGER'S GUIDE TO BETTER

EXIT
INTERVIEWING

Stephen D. Bruce, Ph.D.

BUSINESS & LEGAL REPORTS

BUREAU OF LAW & BUSINESS, INC. • HAZARDOUS WASTE BULLETIN

64 WALL STREET, MADISON, CT 06443-1513

EDITORIAL AND PRODUCTION STAFF:

Managing Editor: Frank R. Abate
Editorial Associates: Gillian M. Akel, Ellen Cananagh, Jo-Ann P. Milici
Design: John F. Kallio

About the Author

Stephen D. Bruce, Ph.D., is an experienced author in the personnel field. Among his titles to date are BLR's best-seller on selection interviewing, *Face to Face: Every Manager's Guide to Better Interviewing,* his book on strategic human resource planning, *Right People, Right Place, Right Time,* and his contributions to BLR's Outplacement and Career Development Workshop, *How to Write Resumes* and *How to Interview Successfully and Get the Job You Want.* In this volume, he brings his practical, straightforward style to the exit interview.

Dr. Bruce brings a unique background to his personnel writing. His immediate personnel background—five years as head of employment for a Fortune 200 firm—is enhanced by a variety of prior experience, including positions as an Army officer, college professor, and retail manager. His background has given him a broad base of experience from which to write—he understands the ins and outs of interviewing as few can, and his here's-how-to-do-it writing style appeals to managers who want to learn how to make every interview count.

Dr. Bruce holds a B.A. from Davidson College, a Master's from the University of Hartford, and a Ph.D. from the University of Oregon.

Contents

Contents

Chapter One

Why Do an Exit Interview?

The exit interview is one of management's most informative tools—and managers who use it well are rewarded with useful information about their organizations that no other source can yield. Yet, in many organizations, the exit interview is neglected or performed in such a way as to produce little, if any, useful information.

This book will show you why the exit interview is so important for your organization, how to prepare for an effective exit interview, and how to conduct one that will give you the information you need.

Why the Exit Interview Is a Special Opportunity

Most managers feel "in tune" with their subordinates; they think they know what the subordinates are thinking, what they are concerned about, and what is important to them. But the fact is that most employees don't share their thoughts and feelings with management, especially their negative feelings, whether these feelings are directed toward the organization or toward the manager. The negative feelings do get expressed in other ways, however. They are shown in morale and attendance problems, attitude changes, and, finally, by departure—"voting with their feet" in the popular parlance.

It's at this point—when an employee has decided to leave the organization—that he or she is most likely to talk frankly about what it is like to work in that organization. People talk very freely in a properly conducted exit interview, and the information gathered can save the organization a surprising amount of money by pinpointing problems early and dramatizing the need for action.

1

How Exit Interviews Differ from Other Interviews

The exit interview differs in a number of important respects from other kinds of interviews. Let's look at some of these differences. Understanding them will help you to conduct productive exit interviews.

● **It's easy to be a lazy interviewer.** In a selection interview, if you fail to do a thorough job, you'll pay the price when the problems begin to show up, because it is "your fault" that the wrong person was hired. But if your exit interview lacks thoroughness, there won't be any immediate reflection on you. Because of this, it's easy to be lazy. Prepare yourself to give your exit interviews the same attention as any other interview; your energy will be well invested.

● **People don't have to talk.** In a selection interview, if people don't talk, they don't get hired, so there's ample pressure on them to respond to your questions. This is not the case in the exit interview—they don't have to talk and they know it. This puts the burden on the interviewer of creating the kind of atmosphere that will encourage communication.

● **The interview can be confrontational and unpleasant.** Particularly in the case where a person has been surprised by his or her termination, emotions can run high. The interviewer may have to deal with the employee's anger and emotional instability, using a counseling approach to promote meaningful communication.

● **The interview can be hard to focus.** Because of two of the factors mentioned above—that the employee doesn't have to talk and that the employee may be emotionally upset—the interview can be hard to focus. In the first case, it's easy for the interview to fall prey to the temptation to have a nice chat and let it go at that. In the second case, it can be hard to get away from the tendency to have a "gripe session" that never gets to the heart of the problem. Your interviewing skills will have to face this challenge.

Your Primary Role

As the exit interviewer, your primary role is to elicit information from the departing employee, information about the termination, about the organization, the department, the position; in short, anything about working for this organization that will help you make the organization more productive. Something is wrong when someone leaves and your role is to identify the problem. It may be a case of hiring the wrong people, treating them poorly, or any of a variety of other things. Your job is to stop it from happening again. Let's probe a little more into the reasons for conducting exit interviews.

PURPOSE OF THE EXIT INTERVIEW

The exit interview usually focuses on both the immediate situation—what brought about this termination—and on more general issues—patterns, problems, and issues as viewed by the departing employee. We find that the exit interview aims in two directions:

first, at reducing the cost of turnover, and second, at identifying other, broader issues (which are often the underlying causes of turnover) which management can address.

Reduce the Cost of Turnover

The cost of excess turnover on an organization is staggering, not only on you, but also on your employees and on the organization.

● **Your time.** Turnover takes a mighty toll on management time. First, there are the direct time consumers of job specification, candidate sourcing, interviewing, and selection. Then there is orientation, welcoming, and training. As one manager put it, each resignation costs you one special project. In the time it takes to bring a new employee on board, you could have completed a project that you'll never get around to.

● **Your career.** Not only won't you get around to those special projects that demonstrate your potential, but your reputation as a manager may suffer also. Why do so many people leave your department?

● **Your other employees.** Turnover starts everyone wondering. Why did that person quit? Why shouldn't I make more money, too? Am I ready to move? And turnover makes your other employees' jobs harder, too. They have to take up the extra workload and they have to help train the new person.

● **Your organization.** When all the individual problems are taken together, the result for the entire organization can be a serious one. Turnover feeds upon itself if morale and confidence are eroded.

Is all turnover bad? No, of course not. First of all, there are some employees that you don't mind losing. Furthermore, most experts agree that a certain amount of turnover is good for an organization. Nevertheless, most organizations have more turnover than they want, and most organizations lose a lot of people that they don't want to lose.

Identify Other Problems

The exit interview has the potential to identify a myriad of other organizational problems that may otherwise remain undetected. Let's look at some of the most important areas.

● **Legal problems.** It is often the case that the more dangerous a problem, the less likely it is to be reported. Potential legal problems like sexual harassment and discrimination frequently remain unreported due to the employee's fear that his or her job may be in jeopardy. The exit interview is the best opportunity to uncover these types of problems. It also offers an opportunity to lessen the likelihood of a lawsuit over one of these issues, or at least to take steps to prepare for a suit if one comes.

● **Specific manager problems.** People are also reluctant to complain about their boss. This is viewed as job-threatening, and not without reason. An exit interview might uncover anything from a drinking or drug problem to abusive management practices.

● **General management problems.** This area includes morale and other employee issues. Are there compensation problems? Do employees feel mistreated in some way? It is important to record these feelings, even if you don't agree that they are well-founded. It's what employees think that is important, not what you think they should think.

Salvage Employees

Under certain circumstances, it may be appropriate to think in terms of "salvaging" an employee. If you have a valued employee leaving, and you have the possibility to resolve whatever problem caused the decision to terminate or resign, you may be able to keep the employee. We'll discuss some of the circumstances under which you might like to do this, but first, a warning.

Caveat: Studies show that most people who are talked into staying on the job after they have tried to resign are likely to leave within six months anyway. Why? Probably because they are viewed with suspicion—they're no longer "part of the team." Nevertheless, there are circumstances in which you will want to try to keep someone.

● **Project completion.** This is probably the most common case. Someone resigns in the middle of a project that only he or she can successfully complete. It may be to your advantage to pay a large bonus or to otherwise entice the person to stay, even though you are sure that he or she will leave soon after the completion of the project.

● **Resigned or terminated in anger.** There may be cases in which the boss or the employee became angry over a small problem or a misunderstanding and acted too hastily. If the employee is a valued one, you may want to try to mediate the situation rather than letting a competent, fully-trained employee go.

● **Problems with the manager.** If you suspect that the employee would get along better under another manager or supervisor, and there are appropriate positions available, consider trying a switch rather than a termination.

● **Job mismatch.** Is it simply a case of a person being in the wrong job? Again, for a valued employee, it may be worth your while to try to transfer the person rather than lose the person.

PURPOSES OF THE EXIT INTERVIEW

Reduce the cost of turnover
- ☐ on your time
- ☐ on your career
- ☐ on your other employees
- ☐ on your organization

Identify other problems
- ☐ legal problems
- ☐ problems with a specific manager
- ☐ general management problems

Salvage employees
- ☐ project completion
- ☐ resigned or terminated in anger
- ☐ problems with manager
- ☐ job mismatch

Other benefits of the exit interview
- ☐ letting the employee vent or sound off
- ☐ part with good feelings
- ☐ set the stage for return

Housekeeping
- ☐ outplacement planning
- ☐ references
- ☐ things to turn in
- ☐ employee questions

Other Benefits of the Exit Interview

There are several other benefits of exit interviews in addition to those previously mentioned.

● **Venting.** Letting people "vent" or "sound off" is often beneficial. People who have been given an opportunity to voice their frustrations are less likely to proceed with a suit or official complaint against the organization. With their complaints off their chests, they are prone to focus on their futures and get on with the business of finding another position.

● **Parting with good feelings.** It just makes good sense to let relationships end with good feelings all around. This person may be a potential customer, and is a source of information about your organization for other people who know he or she worked there. Your other employees will notice this also. Parting with good feelings is so important to the "Big 8" accounting firms that most of them have fully-staffed outplacement offices just to help departing employees find a new position. The payoffs in good will and future business make this well worth the effort.

● **Set the stage for return.** It is not unusual for people to set off after greener pastures, only to find that the grass wasn't greener after all. Such people are often welcomed back, because their knowledge of the company is valued and because it is assumed that having tried "the outside" they will be back for good. Also, to be frank, there's a certain smugness management feels when such people return.

Housekeeping

Finally, there are often a group of administrative actions to take care of in the exit interview. Depending upon how your organization is structured, many of these may be taken care of by another person (in fact, we recommend that this be the practice); however, we'll mention them in this book so that you can be sure that somebody is taking care of them.

● **Outplacement.** If you are offering outplacement services, or the use of a phone or secretary, for example, you may want to clarify just what the organization is going to do, and how long the service will be offered.

● **References.** In certain cases, there will be questions about what the "official" position of the organization will be. Did the person resign? How will the organization answer questions asbout the person's performance?

● **Turn in.** Collection of items such as I.D. cards, credit cards, and equipment may be on your list of things to do.

● **Questions.** Finally, you should be prepared to answer employee questions about continuing benefits, severance, or whatever. If you don't know the answer, be ready with the name of the proper person to contact.

For a detailed discussion of things you might have to cover, see the chapter on what to do in the interview.

KEYS TO A GOOD EXIT INTERVIEW SYSTEM

Here are several pointers about how to establish your exit interview routine and how to choose who does the interview, and where and when it occurs.

Establish a Routine

One of the problems with exit interviews is that they often don't happen unless there is a well-established system for doing them. Here are some suggestions for making sure that the exit interview is an established part of the routine for leaving the organization.

● **Have a policy.** Make the exit interview a mandatory action that is required by organization policy. Then the employee can't forget about it, and the manager can't get away with saying, "Oh, don't worry about it, I took care of it." (See the chapter on policies for samples of three types of policies.)

● **Be consistent.** Use a form or a standard format for your exit interviews. This will help you cover all the territory you want to and will help you organize your conclusions. As we'll see later on, the information you get from exit interviews is often used together with information from previous interviews, and a consistent format helps you to do this.

● **Allow plenty of time.** Schedule your exit interviews formally, that is, don't just say, "Drop by before you leave." Make the exit interview a serious piece of business.

● **Keep careful records.** If your information is to be useful, you'll need careful notes of what people said. It will often be a long time before you are able to use the information.

Who Should Be Interviewed?

We recommend that everyone who leaves your employ be given an exit interview. First of all, this is easiest to handle from a policy standpoint: everyone gets interviewed before leaving the organization. Secondly, you never know where you're going to get important information or good ideas. Finally, as we'll see in a later chapter, to make good use of your exit interview information, you need complete data.

Who Should Do the Exit Interview?

Our recommendation is that someone in the personnel department be assigned this role. There are three reasons for this, capability, perspective, and objectivity.

● **Capability.** Personnel staffers are likely to be skilled in interviewing and counseling techniques. They're much more likely to conduct an interview that elicits useful information.

7

● **Perspective.** The function needs to be centralized so that a person with a perspective on the whole organization performs the exit interviews. A single manager who hears from one employee that the resignation is due to a low salary will probably shrug. But a personnel manager who has heard this four times in the last month will know that something has to be done.

● **Objectivity.** Furthermore, the department manager often doesn't want to hear about problems in the department, and is likely to ignore them. The manager may hear, for instance, that an employee resigned because the job wasn't what was promised. The personnel interviewer will realize that this is a hiring problem, and can take action to be sure that it doesn't happen again.

When Should Two Interviewers Be Involved?

Two interviewers are not normally required. However, it may be wise to have two present if the person has just been terminated and is very upset, or if you suspect that some serious allegations may be made.

When Should You Hold the Exit Interview?

First of all, the most informative interviews are conducted in person shortly before the person leaves. This ensures that the interview will take place and that it will occur when the person is most likely to be frank. Some organizations have tried to conduct exit interviews with questionnaires mailed to the person after he or she leaves the organization, on the theory that after a few weeks away they will be very open. Unfortunately, however, these are often not returned, or if they are, they are filled out without much thought. It takes a face-to-face interview to dig in and get useful information.

For unexpected terminations, when the person is expected to leave immediately after the termination, the exit interview will have to be held on the spot. These will always be difficult, but your skillful interviewing and counseling will help make the situation as pleasant as it can be.

Where Should You Hold the Exit Interview?

The most important thing is to find a place which is private and free from interruptions. Your office or a neutral territory is probably best. Freedom from interruptions is particularly important. The person being interviewed needs to know that the interview is serious. The best way for you to demonstrate that is to set aside time and attention for it.

Coordinating the Two Exit Interviews

As we mentioned above, there are often two separate interviews—one administrative meeting for collecting materials, signing papers, and so on, and one for discussing the work relationship. We strongly recommend this separation of duties. The primary focus of this book is on the information-gathering role of the exit interview; however, both are covered.

The exit interview is an important and cost-effective tool for management, and often, it is the only way to get the information you want. Through it, the organization can learn about itself and show itself how to change for the better. Let's find out how to get ready for an effective exit interview.

Chapter Two

How to Prepare for the Exit Interview

Preparation for the exit interview is every bit as important as preparation for a selection interview—you'll get much more out of it if you do your homework. First, we'll take a look at some general preparation that you can do for all exit interviews and then we'll turn to preparation for the individual exit interview.

FOR ALL EXIT INTERVIEWS

Before you start looking at an individual's situation, be sure that you're armed with the basic information you need for any exit interview.

Know Your Policies

First, be familiar with your organization's policies on exit interviews. Know what the rules and requirements are. Then you will be on firm ground when you make the arrangements for the interview. Second, familiarize yourself with your organization's policies on terminations, severance packages, continuance of benefits, and so on. Then you'll be able to answer questions and you'll be in a better position to understand the situation the person leaving is in.

Use a Form

For the sake of consistency and to avoid forgetting anything important, most managers find that it is helpful to use a form or at least to follow a standard format. Samples of a wide variety of forms are included with this book in the chapter on exit interview forms. Find one there that fits your needs, or create your own, taking the parts of each sample that apply to your situation.

Know Your Organization's Key Concerns

Know what your organization's basic human resource concerns are, and be prepared to discuss them with all exit interviewees. For instance, you might be concerned about the effects of a salary freeze, or a planned down-sizing. Another organization might be particularly concerned about racial discrimination or sexual harassment, or might just have implemented a new performance appraisal or orientation system. Whatever the issues in your organization, prepare yourself to cover them in the interview.

FOR EACH EXIT INTERVIEW

There is also preparation to be done for each individual exit interview. The more you know about the situation beforehand, the more information you are likely to be able to get, and the more meaningful your conclusions and interpretations will be. You should investigate how and why the termination or resignation occurred, other information about the employee that will help you to understand the situation, and also information about other terminations in that department and throughout the organization.

How and Why the Termination Occurred

Finding the real reason for a termination is very important. Be aware that the real cause is often hidden. Many resignations that appear to be voluntary are caused by factors that you should know about and should be doing something about. The typical reasons for termination are the following:

● **Voluntary.** People commonly resign to take another job that appeals to them more, or because they don't like the one they have, or because of family pressures or for any number of other reasons. Naturally, retirement comes in under this heading also. Be sure that you dig for the real reason. If you sense that the termination may not have been as voluntary as it appears to be on the surface, investigate. Be particularly on the lookout for instances of constructive discharge or indications of sexual harassment or discrimination.

● **No-fault.** This covers those situations which the organization is powerless to prevent. Examples of this would be a takeover or merger.

● **Necessary organization action.** This is the case where the termination is not caused by factors the employee can control. For instance, due to financial difficulties, an organization might be forced to close a plant or an office location. Or it might just be forced to cut payroll costs. Changes of personnel requirements can also cause terminations. For instance, automation may result in a loss of jobs, or a switch in product lines might cause the sales force to be cut.

the way of your role of collecting information by setting up an adversary relationship that interferes with good communication.

The next chapter considers what to do during the exit interview.

PREPARATION CHECKLIST

This is a list of items that may need to be explored as you prepare for your exit interviews.

Policies

Are you familiar with your organization's policies about exit interviews?
Are you familiar with your organization's policies on termination, severance, benefits, etc.?

Form

Do you have a special form or clear outline to guide you through the exit interview?

Organization's key concerns

Are you familiar with your organization's key concerns?

How and why the termination occurred

What circumstances brought about this termination?

- ☐ voluntary resignation
- ☐ no-fault
- ☐ necessary organization action
- ☐ chemistry
- ☐ cause
- ☐ arbitrary

Other information about the employee

What was the employee's level of performance?
Are there any problems with the hiring process?
Should the employee's background have provided clues to the problem?
What do other employees say caused this termination?

Information about other terminations

Have others been discharged in similar situations?
Are any patterns developing?

Legal issues

Is there any evidence of legal problems?

- ☐ discrimination
- ☐ sexual harassment
- ☐ constructive discharge
- ☐ abusive discharge
- ☐ implied contract

Chapter Three

What to Do in the Exit Interview

In exit interviewing, a lot depends on the circumstances of the termination. Some people are happy to be leaving, some are sad; some are very bitter and angry. Some are eager to complain about the organization and tell you all about what's wrong with it. Others have decided that they don't want to "burn any bridges," and they won't say anything about the organization except how wonderful it is. Your job is to establish an atmosphere of communication that lets you get a true picture of what the person is thinking and feeling.

Because of this, the exit interview is often a freewheeling conversation, unlike the usually-more-structured selection interview in which you know what you want to talk about. This casual approach is important, but don't let things wander so much that you don't get anywhere. Be flexible, but get through the points that you want to cover.

Perhaps the most important factor in developing the right kind of atmosphere is your listening skills.

Be a Good Listener

Here are four things to concentrate on to make yourself a good listener—and to encourage a free flow of information.

● **Listen—don't talk.** In any kind of interview, the most common mistake is for the interviewer to do most of the talking. This can be because you're nervous, or because you aren't sure just what to ask. Whatever the reason, what's most important is that you won't learn anything by talking yourself. Naturally, you have to participate, but watch yourself, and keep quiet most of the time. A careful plan will usually keep you on the right track.

● **Listen with a pencil.** Take notes as you go. Most experienced interviewers know that they need to jot down just a word or phrase to remind them of what was said. Don't try to take things down verbatim, but make sure that you can remember later when you write up a report.

● **Listen in perspective.** In the back of your mind, keep information about the position this person was in, the boss, and the issues that you think are important in this case. As you listen, you can read between the lines to make your own interpretation of the true picture.

● **Listen with interest.** A little empathy goes a long way toward effective communication. Give the other person your attention and your understanding.

Use Effective Questioning Techniques

The second way to increase the amount of information you get is to use effective questioning techniques. Here are some types of questions to use and some to avoid.

● **Avoid yes/no questions.** Look at this typical interview scenario to see what happens when you use yes/no questions:

Q. Did you like your job here?

A. Yes.

Q. Do you think we have good employee relations?

A. Yes.

Q. Did you think your boss was a tyrant?

A. No.

Clearly, you're not getting any information out of this interview at all. Instead of these yes/no questions, try some open-ended ones.

● **Use open-ended questions.** These are questions that can't be answered with a yes or a no. They start with why or what or how. Let's look at the three questions above changed into open-ended format:

What do you feel about your job here?

How would you characterize our employee relations?

Could you describe your relationship with your boss?

● **Avoid telegraphing.** Telegraphing is letting the person know what answer you expect by the way in which you ask the question. For example:

You're leaving because you found a better job, right?

A more effective question is less directive:

How did you come to decide to leave?

● **Use a probing approach.** To find out how people really feel, you'll often have to probe beyond the first answer. As we mentioned, a lot of people would just as soon not make negative comments; they're happier giving the expected answers and moving on. And that's what will happen if you don't probe a bit. Here's a brief example:

How did you come to decide to leave?

Well, a nice offer came along that I just can't pass up.

This might seem like the real reason, but try a few more questions.

Had you been actively looking for a new position?

Well, yes.

What led you to start looking?

Well, I guess if you really want to know, it was because of my boss. It's probably sexual harassment if I wanted to sue, but it seemed easier to just look for another job.

We're not suggesting that there is some sinister problem behind every termination. But probing for more information is the best way to assure yourself that you're getting the whole story.

● **Echo the answer.** The echo is a time-honored technique for encouraging communication. Here's an example:

How would you characterize your relationship with your boss?

Well, he's not a very good manager.

You say he's not a very good manager?

● **Twist the answer.** Another technique for getting more information is to twist the answer. For instance:

What do you feel about your work here?

I haven't been very happy here.

Would you say that most of the employees are unhappy?

● **Ask for amplification.** This is an obvious approach, but one that is often overlooked. Simply ask the person for more information.

I haven't been very happy here.

Could you give me some specific examples of problems?

● **Try the silent treatment.** Your silence can be a very effective request for information. People are uncomfortable with silence and they are likely to try to fill it—often with important information.

Use these techniques for listening and for asking questions. They work, and they will make your exit interviews much more meaningful. Now let's turn to the question of what to do in your exit interviews.

THE EXIT INTERVIEW

Frequently, the exit interview will dictate its own path, and to keep the information flowing you'll have to follow it. But experience shows that a basic outline helps. First of all, if things bog down, you'll have someplace to go next. Second, you'll know what you want to cover and you won't later realize that you forgot to discuss something important. You'll find our suggested outline below. It flows from a relaxing introduction through the immediate situation to broader concerns, and it is designed to encourage the exchange of information.

Outline of a Typical Exit Interview

Introduction

The Immediate Situation

Employment History

Organization Concerns

Comments & Suggestions

Housekeeping & Administrative Details

Closing

Let's look at each section of the interview and see what to cover and how to cover it most effectively.

INTRODUCTION

In the introduction, you'll want to put the person at ease and set the stage for what is to come. Here are two pointers:

● **Create an informal atmosphere.** In the exit interview situation, a formal atmosphere tends to stifle open communication. A formal atmosphere suggests that this is merely a formality. Instead, you'd like just the opposite. A little "small talk" will help you get started.

● **Explain the role of the interview.** It helps people to know what's coming. As an example, you might say:

> *Today I'd like to chat with you about why you're leaving, what thoughts and suggestions you have about our organization, and finally, we have a few housekeeping details to take care of. We don't like to lose good people like you, and anything you can tell us about your experience here will help us understand how to do our jobs better.*

THE IMMEDIATE SITUATION

Your first area of discussion is usually the immediate situation. This is the logical starting place, and it's what the person you are interviewing expects to discuss. Here are some suggested questions for the most common termination situations.

Voluntary Terminations

Most people who have resigned voluntarily are willing to discuss their situations quite openly. Let's look at several common situations and see what approach to use.

● **Resigned to accept new position.** This is the most common situation you'll face. These situations appear to be straightforward, and the temptation is to rush through the exit interview because the situation "is obvious." But remember two things. First of all, there is something that led this person to accept a new position, and you need to know what it was. Second, these people are the ones you most care about leaving—they're the ones that are attractive to other organizations, and therefore, probably the ones you'd least like to lose.

> *Tell me about your new position.*
>
> *What attracts you about the new position?*
>
> *How did you find out about your new position?*
>
> *Did you find them or did they find you?*
>
> *What new responsibilities will you have?*
>
> *Will you get a salary increase?*
>
> *When did you decide to leave this organization?*
>
> *Did any specific event make you decide to leave?*

● **Resigned to find new position.** People in this situation usually say something like: "Oh, it was just time to move on" or "I didn't see much future here" or "I wanted to devote my full energy to a search for a new job." This situation should arouse your suspicions a bit. Although it's not unheard of, when the termination is truly voluntary, most people try to secure a new position before leaving the old one. Usually when someone resigns without having secured a new position, there is some factor that is forcing or at least encouraging the resignation.

What are your plans for the future?

Have you been looking for a new job?

Are you going to look for the same kind of position?

How will you go about your job search?

Will you look for the same kind of organization?

When did you make the decision to leave?

What specific factors led you to this decision?

● **Resigned within two years of hiring.** This case should get some special investigation because these terminations are very costly to the organization. The person has barely begun to be productive by the time of termination. Particularly when someone has been with the organization less than one year, you should probe reasons very carefully. In addition to asking about things that led to the decision to leave, ask questions that help you to evaluate whether this person should ever have been in this job, and whether training and orientation were adequate.

Were you doing what you expected to be doing?

Did the job turn out to be what you had been led to believe it would be?

How soon after arriving here did you sense that there was something wrong?

Did you feel like a round peg in a square hole?

What attracted you to this job in the first place?

Involuntary Terminations

This situation can be quite different from the voluntary one. Your person may be bitter, angry, even hostile. Your job is to break through to get the information you want—because you don't want this happening again. You may have to listen to some harsh talk, but it's worth it if you can get to the root of the problem.

I remember when we last talked things were fine. What happened?

How would you describe what led to this situation?

Would your boss agree with that assessment?

What could you have done differently?

When did you first realize that there were problems brewing?

Was this a surprise to you?

Was this a logical decision for the organization to have made?

What Are the Real Reasons?

Remember that many people would prefer to avoid this question and will offer a pat answer about "a great new opportunity." Persevere and probe to be sure that you're getting to the real reasons. Later on in the interview, you'll probably find out more about the reasons, as you discuss the person's work history and get the person's suggestions and comments.

First, there are several clues that should alert you to possible hidden problems. For instance, if the new position offers a lower salary than the current one, or if the responsibilities are fewer, you should be probing for more information. These indicators are not foolproof, but they often do point to some kind of difficulty.

Here are some questions that will help you to see the kinds of underlying situations that may have caused "voluntary" termination.

Is a performance problem due to lack of ability or lack of interest?

Is this the right person in the wrong job?

Is the person overqualified or underqualified for the position?

Was the person adequately trained?

Are there job difficulties beyond the employee's control?

Is there a management problem you should be aware of?

Note that the real reason may not be apparent early in the interview. As you talk more and more, however, you may start to get hints that will let you get to the real reason later in the interview.

At some point in the discussion above, you'll find yourself ready to move naturally into the question of what the organization could have done differently.

What Could the Organization Have Done?

What you will ask here will depend upon the specific situation. Here are some examples of the type of questions you might want to ask:

What could we have done differently?

Do you think that a better training program would have helped?

If you had been assigned to a different manager, would that have changed things?

If your salary had been higher, would you have been more likely to stay?

Should the personnel department have done something about this situation?

EMPLOYMENT HISTORY

Again, you'll tailor your questions to the specific situation. If you are interviewing a five-year employee, don't concentrate on the orientation process; with a six-month employee, do. Here are some sample questions about management and about personnel.

Management

Here you'll concentrate on the general management of your organization as it affected this person. You are interested in how the policies and practices of your managers were involved in the termination.

● **Immediate manager.** The relationship between the employee and his or her immediate boss is always an important factor.

> *How would you characterize your relationship with your boss?*
>
> *What is your boss's style of management?*
>
> *How could your boss have helped you more?*
>
> *Did you feel that you were given enough training?*
>
> *Did you feel that you had enough responsibility?*

● **Position.** Sometimes the real problem is caused by a mismatch between the person and the position, or by something inherent in the position that makes it difficult for anyone to do it well.

> *Do you think this was the right position for you?*
>
> *What are the problems that a person in this position faces?*
>
> *Do you think the next person in this position will have problems also?*
>
> *Are there any changes that you would recommend?*
>
> *What's the most difficult thing about this job?*
>
> *What kind of training is best for this position?*
>
> *What's the worst thing about this position?*
>
> *What's the best thing about this position?*

● **Department.** Next, broaden the scope of your questioning to cover the department. This immediate environment in which the person worked has a great impact on ability to do the job well.

> *What can you tell me about your co-workers?*

What's the working atmosphere like there?

How did your position tie in with the others in the department?

Was there anything your co-workers could have done differently?

What's the biggest problem in your department?

Do you think that others in the department will leave soon?

What changes would you recommend in the operation of this department?

● **Organization as a whole.** Finally, take a look at the organization as a whole. See if you can pinpoint any specific areas that are causing problems.

How would you describe the culture here?

What's most important to management here?

Is this a good place to work?

Is there good communication from upper management?

With which other departments did you work?

Does everybody seem to pull together for the good of the whole organization?

Personnel Processes

The other general area to cover is the personnel processes. Depending on the position involved and the person involved, you may want to cover some or all of the following.

● **The personnel department.** Particularly if you are with the personnel department, you'll want to assess its role in this situation, and what it could have done to prevent the problem.

How do you view the personnel department here?

Did you visit the personnel department when you realized that there was a problem?

What could our department have done to make the situation better?

● **The hiring process.** When someone leaves the organization, whatever the reason, it's wise to take a look at the hiring process that brought the person on board. You'd like to know if there is some way in which the problem could have been foreseen and prevented.

How was this position described to you when you were being hired?

What was the biggest surprise you found when you started work?

How would you characterize your orientation activities?

How long did it take for you to feel "part of the team"?

Were any promises made at the time of your employment that were not fulfilled?

Is there anything we should have done differently?

● **Training and development.** The kind of training and development that a person receives can often make the difference between success and failure on the job.

Can you describe your initial training period?

Was there anything about your job that you never understood?

Would more or better training have made a difference?

Is there anything in particular that we should do with the next person who takes this position?

● **Benefits and compensation.** People often offer inadequate benefits and compensation as a reason for leaving. You'd like to find out whether there are real problems here that may cause others to leave.

How do you think our compensation compares with other organizations?

How does our benefit program compare?

Is there something particularly attractive about your new position's benefits?

What is the overall feeling here about compensation and benefits?

● **Future opportunities.** Another common reason for leaving an organization is perceived lack of future opportunity. Be especially aware of the situation where there *was* opportunity, but someone left because he or she didn't *think* there was such an opportunity.

What would you expect would have been your next assignment had you stayed?

Did you talk to your boss about future opportunities?

Will opportunities be better in your new position?

ORGANIZATION CONCERNS

Next, turn the discussion to general organization concerns. These may be normal issues like morale and communication, or some special concern on which your management is concentrating.

General Issues

These are the kinds of broad management issues that any organization is concerned about. Some of the most common are the following.

● **Morale.** Morale is a major concern of every manager. Poor morale is one of the biggest contributors to low productivity, and any problems that you can turn up here are important to know about.

> *What's the nicest thing about being an employee of this organiztion?*
>
> *How would you characterize morale of the employees here?*
>
> *Do you expect that others will be following you out of the organization?*
>
> *What factors contribute to low morale here?*

● **Communication.** Communication is another area that often causes problems. Employees often know surprisingly little about what is important to management.

> *How well informed were you about management's goals for this organization?*
>
> *Do you feel that communication between you and your boss was adequate?*
>
> *How would you characterize our communication program here?*
>
> *What would you like to have known more about?*
>
> *How could we have improved our communications program?*

● **Loyalty and esprit.** These are elusive qualities, but qualities that are important for any organization.

> *How do you feel about leaving this organization?*
>
> *Would you recommend this organization to a friend?*
>
> *What will you miss most about this organization?*

Particular Issues

Be sure that you cover those particular issues that your organization is concerned about. These might have to do with a recent attitude survey, or a recent change in policy, or a concern about drugs, or any number of other issues. In general, you'll want to see how that issue affected the particular employee, and whether the employee has any general observations about the situation. The departing employee will often give you some information that won't be available anywhere else.

SUGGESTIONS & COMMENTS

Although you've probably covered most everything with the questions suggested above, be sure to allow some time for the employee's suggestions and comments. You may find that you've missed something important.

> *Do you have any other suggestions for us?*

What single thing could this organization do to improve employee relations?

Is there anything else I should know about?

HOUSEKEEPING & ADMINISTRATIVE DETAILS

There may be administrative details to be taken care of before the person can leave. As we've mentioned, these are usually covered by another person, or at another time. We've included a checklist at the end of this chapter for you to go over, just to be sure that someone is taking care of these items.

EMPLOYEE QUESTIONS

Finally, be sure to give the employee a chance to ask any questions he or she may have. These can range from technical questions about benefits, to questions about outplacement services, to questions about what kind of reference will be given. If you don't know the answer, direct the person to the department that can answer the question, or tell the person that you'll find out the answer. This consideration will go a long way toward making the termination as pleasant a process as possible.

CLOSING

When you have accomplished what you wanted, bring the interview to a close. Be sincere in wishing the person good luck.

WRITE YOUR REPORT

As soon as possible after the conclusion of the exit interview, write up your report. If you wait too long, you'll forget what was said and your notes will be less likely to help you remember. As we'll see in the next chapter, good written reports are essential for making effective use of the information you get out of the exit interview.

ADMINISTRATIVE CHECKLIST

This is a list of items that may need to be covered when an employee leaves your organization. Naturally, you won't need to cover each of these with every employee, but running down the list will help you be sure that you don't forget anything important.

References

What references will be given to future employers who contact you?

Did this employee resign or was he or she terminated?

Is this employee eligible for unemployment insurance?

Services

What services will be provided to this person after he or she leaves?

- ☐ formal outplacement program
- ☐ counseling
- ☐ help with resume preparation
- ☐ instruction on interviewing and jobfinding techniques
- ☐ secretarial services
- ☐ phone answering

Compensation and Financial

Employment contracts

If the person is under contract, how will the contract be satisfied?

Compensation

What salary questions have to be answered?

- ☐ severance amount
- ☐ salary owed
- ☐ bonuses earned
- ☐ commissions earned
- ☐ accrued and unused vacation
- ☐ personal days unused
- ☐ sick leave unused

Pension and savings programs

What arrangements must be made?

☐ vesting of pension benefits

☐ retirement program

☐ social security benefits

☐ thrift and savings plan funds

☐ stock options

☐ profit sharing

☐ loans, credit extended

Expense reports

Are any expense reports outstanding?

Benefits

Many benefit issues will need to be resolved. Here are some of the most common:

Relocation

Are any payments owed to the person?

Are funds from bridge loans owed to the organization?

Are mortgage differential payments in effect?

If this person was recently relocated, will you move him or her back?

Insurance

What are the policies for continuance of insurance programs?

☐ life

☐ health

☐ travel

Perquisites

What policies govern the continuation of perquisites such as the following?

☐ physicals at organization's expense

☐ tuition aid for the employee for courses in progress

☐ scholarship continuation for children of employees

☐ financial and tax planning services

☐ automobiles owned by the organization

☐ club memberships

☐ subscriptions

☐ professional association dues

Return of Company Property

Are there items which must be turned in before the employee can leave?

☐ credit cards

☐ identification cards

☐ keys

☐ equipment

Security

Are there security issues concerning this position?

Does this person need to be reminded of organization policy?

Are there patent, royalty, or invention rights issues?

Ongoing Work Issues

Are there special issues that arise from this person's position or work?

☐ replacements for person on committees or project staffs

☐ scheduled seminars which another employee should attend

☐ corporate records and forms on which this person is the signatory

☐ incomplete projects which must be finished

☐ reports which are required

☐ briefings on continuing projects

Chapter Four

How to Use Exit Interview Information

The information you gain from well-executed exit interviews is information that can be very important in your human resources management program. What's particularly important to recognize about this information is that you can't always use it right away; in fact, you may choose not to use it at all. Before we talk specifically about using exit interview information, let's consider a few important caveats.

● **Use information to solve problems.** Your role is to identify problems, not create them. Be careful with negative information that you gain in your exit interviews and be sure that you're going to accomplish a useful purpose by relating your findings.

● **Consider the source.** Is the person who's leaving a valued employee, respected by all in the organization? Or is it someone everyone thinks the organization is better off without?

● **Take it with a grain of salt.** People in the throes of leaving an organization are often under a lot of stress. They may well overstate the case, or even lie about a situation. The important thing is to be sure not to automatically assume that everything said is true.

Their Word against the Manager's

This is another important characteristic of exit interviewing interpretation. Some managers take criticism well and are able to use it to improve their management ability. But many managers are not able to do that. They are more likely to become defensive and make light of a terminating employee's critical comment. Let's look at an example:

You've just completed an exit interview with an employee who resigned. It's a person that you hired and you are sure she is capable and has been doing a good job. She has told you that the only reason she is leaving is that her manager is abusive and that he makes degrading comments that she considers to be harassment. You mention this to the manager. His response? "Well, she never did a full day's work anyway—no wonder she thought I was unreasonable." He chuckles, and that's that.

Generally, one complaint is not very influential; but when the complaints start mounting up, they can be very powerful. You'll have a strong case that will be very hard to refute when you can approach this same manager or your boss and say, "This is the fifth person to resign from that department in the last six months, and every one of them said he or she left because the manager was abusive. And three of the people were women who complained of harassment." Everyone will see clearly that this manager's style is costing the organization a lot of money, to say nothing of the morale problems and the legal hassles that will eventually emerge.

It is because of such a situation that it is so important to keep good records and to refer to previous exit interviews when you prepare for new ones. Many of your most effective gains will come from information that is collected over time.

WHERE TO GO WITH YOUR INFORMATION

Here are some pointers about where you can go with exit information. You will have to exercise your judgment about where to go in each case.

● **The file.** A copy of every report should go into your files. As we've mentioned above, it is important to be able to refer back to these materials.

● **The manager.** For minor problems, or for problems that you and the manager have discussed before, go directly to the manager. For example, you might have an employee say he felt that he was never trained adequately. This you could share directly with the manager. Or, you and the manager may have been talking about interviewing skills. If he or she just lost another new employee, it may be the right time to suggest an interviewing course.

● **Your boss.** For more serious matters, you should probably check with your boss. First of all, he or she may know more about the situation than you do. There may be problems of which you are unaware that bear upon the situation. Also, if you're talking about serious problems, your boss needs to be aware of what you are doing, because there may be some serious reactions to your comments.

● **Your organization attorney.** For problems which seem to have serious legal implications, you may want to check with your organization's attorney. For instance, if an employee threatens a suit or a complaint, it may be time to call the lawyers in. Naturally, in a case like this, your boss should also be involved.

SUMMARY

Your exit interview is a powerful tool in personnel management. During your exit interviews you will hear about a lot of situations that you would otherwise never have known about. And, with a consistent program of exit interviewing, you'll be able to solve the problems you uncover. Your role as exit interviewer is an important one, for you and for your organization.

The next chapter will tell you what you need to know about exit interview policies, and the final chapter will cover exit interview forms. In both chapters, you will find several examples that will help you to develop policies and forms of your own.

Good Interviewing!

Chapter Five

Exit Interview Policies

As we mentioned earlier, having a clear and official policy which governs the exit interview is important. For most people leaving an organization, whether the choice was the employee's or the organization's, the exit interview is a low priority. Without a clear requirement that they be performed, many exit interviews will never take place. It's simply too easy to "not quite get around to it."

In this chapter, we'll discuss the main things that such policies should cover, and several other points to keep in mind. The end of the chapter consists of three sample policies. Feel free to use them as they are or to revise them to suit your particular needs.

WHAT TO COVER IN YOUR POLICY

Some companies simply attach a copy of the exit interview form to their general policy on terminations (see "standard" policy on accompanying pages). But if you intend to write out a separate policy statement on exit interviews, here are the points you should try to cover:

● **Mandatory.** The policy should require that the interview be performed, and it should indicate to which employees this requirement applies.

● **Purpose.** As clearly as possible, state what you see as the purpose for exit interviews. It may be to discover the real reasons for the employee's decision to leave, or to get the employee to reconsider his or her decision.

● **Interviewer.** Who normally conducts the exit interview? It is usually someone from the personnel office, although it may be the immediate supervisor or department head, or even a member of top management. Should two members of management be present? It may be wise if you expect some problems.

- **When the interview is held.** Most exit interviews are scheduled as close to the time of the employee's actual departure as possible. But if the termination is voluntary, it may be held a day or two in advance.

- **Interview format.** If you want to, you can outline the approach you want the interviewer to take and the points you want covered. Some firms include tips for interviewers on how to avoid defensiveness, how to get the employee to open up, how to remain objective when the employee criticizes the firm or his supervisor, etc.

- **Interview form or questionnaire.** It is common to have either the interviewer or the departing employee (or in some cases, both) fill out an exit interview form. Sometimes the form simply replaces the interview itself, although obviously it isn't going to elicit the same kind of information as a face-to-face discussion. If your company uses such a form, you can attach it to your policy statement.

OTHER POINTS TO CONSIDER

Exit interviews are a waste of time if both parties aren't willing to be candid. For this reason, many companies train the individuals who regularly conduct exit interviews in how to handle what is often a highly charged situation. Whether or not such training is available in your firm, you will want to give careful consideration to the following:

- **Your company's turnover rate.** If turnover is traditionally high in your firm, exit interviews may hold the key to finding out why. Careful attention should be paid to writing the policy so that this information is brought to light. Write the policy so that it requires that written records of what is said during these interviews be maintained and reviewed from time to time to discover patterns in employees' responses.

- **Past experience with exit interviews.** If exit interviews in the past have turned into explosive and counterproductive arguments, or if employees have often been too hesitant to reveal their true feelings about terminating, perhaps it's time to revamp your policy and give interviewers more guidance on how to handle such reactions. If interviewers feel that much is learned but little is done with the information that comes out of the exit interview, then this too should be remedied. Have your policy committee talk to the individuals who have conducted these interviews to get their opinions on what might be done.

- **Sensitivity to EEO.** The exit interview often reveals that discrimination—or at least the possibility of discrimination—has played a role in the decision to terminate an employee or in the employee's decision to leave. It is common for supervisors to base a termination on pretext. For example, suppose that a female employee is fired for insubordination and unsatisfactory job performance—both justifiable motives for discharge. But in talking to her during the exit interview, the interviewer discovers that she has regularly received satisfactory performance reviews from her supervisor, and that the only unsatisfactory rating came after she filed a sex discrimination complaint with the EEOC. Your policy might mention that top management and counsel should be alerted immediately to the possibility of a discrimination suit based on retaliation for filing a complaint.

The three sample policies that follow reflect three different approaches to establishing a policy on exit interviews. All three are fairly common, and their categorization as "strict," "standard," and "progressive" is simply an indication of how far they go in dealing with the content of exit interviews and the manner in which they should be conducted. The "strict" policy consists of brief paragraphs stating that departing employees will be interviewed by a member of the personnel department and that the resulting information will be recorded on an appropriate form. The "standard" policy is actually only an exit interview form attached to a broader policy on terminations in general. The "progressive" policy is probably the most complete and the most helpful in terms of offering the necessary guidance on how to conduct the interview itself.

Caution: Recall the earlier discussion of negligent evaluation. If your exit interview suggests the employee was not properly evaluated, properly trained, properly supervised, etc., and if your handbook or conduct suggests that all these things will be done properly, then you may be liable for negligence. Again, you must follow up on the information obtained and correct the situation after notifying management and your attorney.

white

Subject: **Exit Interview**
Organization: Anonymous
Example of: Strict Policy

EFFECTIVE DATE: _____   SUPERSEDES: _____

Policy applies to: All employees

Form required is: Form E4

Action office is: Personnel Department

Exceptions require signature of: Vice-President, Personnel

POLICY:

Before they receive their final checks, departing employees will be interviewed by a member of the Personnel Office to determine the exact reasons for termination.

When desirable, an attempt may be made to salvage employees by transfer or by attempting to rectify conditions causing dissatisfaction.

The exit interview form will be filled out by the interviewer and made part of the Personnel Office files.

Subject: **Exit Interviews**
Organization: Anonymous
Example of: Standard policy

It is the policy of this organization that all terminating employees will complete this form on or before their last day of work.

EXIT INTERVIEW FORM

Code: U = Unsatisfactory   G = Good

         F = Fair   E = Excellent

         S = Satisfactory

Please check the one that most nearly applies:

	U	F	S	G	E
1. Generally speaking, I would rate this company as a _____ place to work.	[]	[]	[]	[]	[]
2. I feel that company policies and procedures are	[]	[]	[]	[]	[]
3. Working conditions, rest rooms, and physical facilities here are	[]	[]	[]	[]	[]
4. As compared to other companies, our benefits package is	[]	[]	[]	[]	[]
5. My understanding of my fringe benefits is	[]	[]	[]	[]	[]
6. The level of concern for employees here is	[]	[]	[]	[]	[]
7. Management's willingness to make corrections and changes is	[]	[]	[]	[]	[]
8. Pay levels at this company are generally	[]	[]	[]	[]	[]
9. The extent to which I understand the basis of my rate of pay is	[]	[]	[]	[]	[]
10. The amount of training I received when I first came here was	[]	[]	[]	[]	[]
11. The extent to which training enables me to do a better job and increase my pay is	[]	[]	[]	[]	[]
12. My understanding of the duties and responsibilities of my job is	[]	[]	[]	[]	[]
13. My understanding of what performance standards I am expected to meet is	[]	[]	[]	[]	[]
14. The extent to which I feel "tuned in" on what's happening throughout the company as a whole is	[]	[]	[]	[]	[]
15. The extent to which I am informed ahead of time regarding changes that affect my work is	[]	[]	[]	[]	[]

                                                          U   F   S   G   E

16. When I do a job well, the recognition   [] [] [] [] []
     I receive is

17. My supervisor's willingness to listen   [] [] [] [] []
     to my problems and help me when I have
     questions is

18. The extent to which I am encouraged by   [] [] [] [] []
     my supervisor to offer suggestions and
     improvements in work methods is

19. The respect and confidence I have in   [] [] [] [] []
     my supervisor are

20. The extent to which I have the   [] [] [] [] []
     opportunity to use or develop my full
     potential is

21. I regard my chances for promotion and   [] [] [] [] []
     increased pay as

22. The level of cooperation among the   [] [] [] [] []
     employees in my department is

23. Did you have a performance review with
     your supervisor at least once a year?   Yes____ No____

24. Did you have training sessions?   Yes____ No____
     If so, who conducted them? _____
     How often were they held? _____

25. What additional training would you have wanted?
     _____

     _____

26. Which employee benefits did you feel were the most
     valuable? _____

     _____
     Why? _____

27. What did you like most about working here?
     _____

     _____

28. What did you like least about working here?

_____

_____

29. What are your suggestions for improving this company as a place to work?

_____

_____

_____

_____

Reason for termination _____

_____

SIGNATURE _____

Subject: **Exit Interview**
Organization: Anonymous
Example of: Progressive Policy

Every employee leaving the Company is to be extended the courtesy of a final interview with a member of management to whom this responsibility is delegated.

A. Exit Interview Form

The Exit Interview Form must be completed by the terminating employee's supervisor and submitted to the person responsible for maintenance of personnel files.

B. Exit Interview Procedure

1. The exit interview, conducted by the Personnel Manager or designated staff member, is to be held:

In the event of a release, on the final day of employment. The employee should not return to work following the interview; therefore, the time of the interview is to be set accordingly; or

In the event of a voluntary resignation or retirement, the exit interview may take place one or more days prior to the date of the termination.

2. When the work of a probationary or temporary employee has been good, a compliment regarding his or her performance is in order. Such employees should be told that they will be called for work again when it is available. In the case of employees whose work has not been satisfactory, do not encourage hopes of securing reemployment at a later date.

3. Make an effort to "sell the employee off the job." If the reason for release is unsatisfactory performance, do not use business conditions as an excuse to the employee. Refer to the corrective interviews which have taken place and point out that an opportunity to improve has been provided. In order to preserve self-confidence and self-respect, advise that although results on this job were unsatisfactory, it does not mean that a different line of work would also prove to be unsatisfactory.

    Point out the employee's favorable qualities with the suggestion that if properly directed they may provide considerable success elsewhere. Leave the employee with the thought that the Company is anxious to help and that this release is to the employee's own advantage.

4. Do not discuss details with the employee in cases involving unsatisfactory references, suspicion of misconduct, etc.

5. If the employee is leaving voluntarily, determine as accurately as possible the real reason for leaving. If the employee is leaving to work elsewhere, attempt to find out the name of the company, type of work, rate of pay, and how the job was obtained.

    Discuss any factors or conditions which might be affecting the efficiency, performance, and morale of the remaining employees which may necessitate corrective action by the Company.

    Discuss briefly the employee's record in the department as to work, attitude, and deportment. Question the employee in order to draw out any comments, complaints, and grievances the employee may have regarding the job, the department, and the Company, provided there is not a union organizing campaign in progress at the time. If there is such a campaign, confer with the president prior to conducting the exit interview.

6. Advise the employee of matters such as final pay, vacation pay, Company benefits, reinstatement policy, unemployment compensation (if requested by employee), and federal old-age benefits (in retirement cases).

7. Explain the Company's reemployment policy to the employee.

8. Explain group life and health insurance conversion, where appropriate.

9. Advise the employee of the date on which life and hospitalization plan coverage terminates, where appropriate.

10. Ensure that any Company property or material in the employee's possession has been returned.

11. Obtain the address at which the employee can be reached for the purpose of directing Form W-2 or for any other reason.

12. Sign the employee's time-card record to indicate to the paymaster that the employee has completed the exit interview.

13. In circumstances which might prove embarrassing to either the employee or the Company, ensure that the employee receives whatever money is due and leaves the building immediately. In such cases, do not let the employee return to his department.

Chapter Six

Exit Interview Forms

The form is the heart of any personnel system or process; in the popular vernacular, the form is "where the action is." The exit interviewing form's function is to collect information. The effectiveness of the exit interviewing system is based on that information. When that information is missing, or inaccurate, the system fails. At the end of this chapter, there is a collection of forms used by organizations across the country in their termination and exit interviewing programs. Let's see how to use them to create our own form.

How Do You Benefit from Other Organizations' Forms?

Basically, it's the old story—why reinvent the wheel? Other personnel managers have already designed your form, and they've already solved your problems. The solutions are right here in this book, in the forms that your colleagues submitted as examples of forms that work for them.

● **Save time and money.** All the hard, time-consuming drudgery of designing and testing forms has already been done for you. Devote your energy to implementing the system.

● **Compare one system to another.** Look at several ways to collect the information you need, and then choose the best way for you.

● **Find things you might have missed.** If someone else needed a certain piece of information, you may need it also.

● **Base your form on a form that works.** The forms in this book are all user-tested in the field. People can fill them out, and the "bugs" are out of them.

Finally, realize that when you look at the form, you can understand the system. As you analyze another organization's form, you can see what the thrust of their system is, what information they are trying to collect, and what they will be using it for. Evaluating the forms is helpful for more than just form design—it can help you understand your system better, too.

HOW TO DESIGN FORMS

Now let's turn to form design. We recommend the following six-step system for designing your forms.

The Six Steps of Form Design

Step 1. Understand the purpose of the form

Step 2. Trace the path of the form

Step 3. List the data the form should collect

Step 4. Adapt a form

Step 5. Test the form

Step 6. Implement the form

You will find each step of the system described below.

Step #1: Understand the Purpose of the Form

Before designing your form, be sure that you know why you need the form. Ask yourself these questions:

What is the overall purpose of the form?

What specific uses will the information be put to?

Step #2: Think How the Form Will Be Used

Think through the development of the form and the actual physical path that the form will follow when in use. Answer these questions:

Who will design, order, stock, and distribute the form?

Who will fill the form out?

Who will see the form after it is filled out?

Who will review the form?

Who will act on the contents of the form?

Who will file and maintain the form?

How many copies of the form are required?

Step #3: List the Data the Form Should Collect

Without thinking about the format of the form, just list each piece of information that you want the form to collect. Then ask these questions:

Will this information satisfy the purpose of the form?

Will the people filling out the form have this information?

Will the people using the form be able to act based on the information on the form?

Is the information available elsewhere?

Step #4: Adapt a Form

When you are satisfied that you know why you need the form, how it will be used, and what information will be requested, then you are ready to adapt a form.

Spend time with the forms in this book. All the forms are from successful organizations and all the forms are actually in use today. They work. As you review them, ask yourself these questions:

How do other people request the information that I need?

Which way of collecting information is the easiest way?

Which form is the most appealing to the person who will fill it out?

● **Adapt a form wholesale.** You may find a form that does exactly what you want—use it just as it is! Be sure, though, that the form will accomplish what you want.

● **Adapt part of a form.** You may find a form that is close to what you need, but needs minor modifications. Add the particular parts that you need, paying careful attention to maintaining consistency with the original form.

● **Combine several forms.** You may decide that you need to combine the parts of several different forms to get just the one that completely fits your particular requirements. Again, pay close attention to the consistency between individual parts.

Step #5: Test the Form

This is a very important step. No matter how carefully you have designed your form, there may be a bug or two in it. It is far better to discover these in a limited test than after the form is fully implemented. Have a few of the people who will be filling out the form give it a try. Watch them as they work on the form. When they pause or hesitate, you'll note a possible problem. If they have to ask questions, they're pointing out an area that may need clarification. After field testing, rework the form if necessary, and then put it into limited use. Only after it proves successful should it be implemented.

Step #6: Implement the Form

By following the testing approach above, you know that your form will work. Put it into use. Here are a few pointers:

Be sure that an adequate supply of forms is available.

Be sure that instructions for filling out the form are clear.

Provide training sessions if you think that people will need assistance the first time around.

Be sure that it is clear who should fill out the form, when it is due, who it should be forwarded to, and where it is to be filed.

That's it. Follow the six steps and you'll create a great form every time.

About the Sample Forms

On the pages which follow, you'll find a variety of sample forms. We've divided the forms into three groups: first, those that are specifically exit interview forms; second, those that are resignation forms; and, third, those that are separation forms. All should be helpful to you in considering the design of your forms. On the next page, you'll find a list of the forms, followed by the forms themselves.

Table of Sample Forms

Exit Interview Forms

1. Exit Interview Form
2. Exit Interview
3. Exit Interview
4. Exit Interview
5. Exit Interview
6. Exit Interview
7. Exit Interview
8. Exit Interview
9. Exit Interview
10. Exit Interview
11. Exit Interview
13. Exit Questionnaire
14. Exit Questionnaire
15. Post Employment Survey

Resignation Forms

16. Notice of Resignation
17. Letter of Resignation
18. Resignation Statement
19. Resignation Form

Separation Forms

20. Information Release for Reference Checks
21. Employee Separation
22. Termination Report
23. Departure Processing
24. Involuntary Termination Review
25. Employee Termination Routing Form
26. Termination Check-off List
27. Termination Statement

1. Exit Interview Form

A Federal Savings and
Loan Association

EXIT INTERVIEW FORM

_____   _____   _____
Conducted with (Name, Title)   Date   Conducted by (Name, Title)

1. For what reasons are you leaving the institution? _____
    _____
    _____

2. What is your understanding of the events which have led to separation? (Cover this,
    if employee was subject to disciplinary procedure.) _____
    _____
    _____

3. What is your opinion of the supervision you received? _____
    _____
    _____

4. What did you most like and dislike about the institution and its policies? _____
    _____
    _____

5. What do you recommend that the institution change? How? _____
    _____
    _____

6. What is your opinion of working conditions in the institution? _____
    _____
    _____

7. How do you feel about the pay? Benefits? _____
    _____
    _____

8. What is your opinion about the training you received? _____
    _____
    _____

9. Do you believe that appropriate opportunities for advancement were available? _____
    _____
    _____

10. Have you obtained a new job? Yes _____   No _____
    If yes, would you please tell us:
    Employer's Name: _____
    Address: _____
    Position Title: _____ Starting Salary: _____

11. What do you see as most attractive about the new job? _____
    _____

_____   _____
Interviewee's Signature   Interviewer's Signature

FM 745-0520-6

2. Exit Interview

EXIT INTERVIEW

This form must be made out personally by the terminating employe's immediate Supervisor or the Department Head and forwarded to the Personnel Department immediately upon completion. If any information is vague or incomplete, the form will be returned.

NAME _____   SERVICE DATE _____

ADDRESS _____   LAST DAY WORKED _____

CITY, STATE _____   TERMINATION DATE _____

EMPLOYE NUMBER _____   LENGTH OF SERVICE____ (Years)____ (Months)

PRESENT POSITION _____

DEPARTMENT _____

SUPERVISOR _____   SERVICE ALLOWANCE $_____

RESIGNATION (Check One)

_____ Secured Better Position
_____ Dissatisfied (Type of Work)
_____ Dissatisfied (Salary)
_____ Dissatisfied (Supervisor)
_____ Dissatisfied (Working Conditions)
_____ Dissatisfied (Living Conditions)
_____ Generally Dissatisfied (Explain)
_____ Poor Health or Physical Condition
_____ Returned to School
_____ Leaving the District
_____ Pregnancy
_____ Family or Personal Circumstances
_____ Marriage
_____ Early Retirement
_____ Temporary Employe
_____ Mutual Agreement (Company/Employe)

DISCHARGE (Check One)

_____ Unsatisfactory Performance
_____ Absenteeism or Tardiness
_____ Lack of Ability
_____ Inability to do Work
_____ Insubordination
_____ Lack of Cooperation
_____ Rules Violation
_____ Dishonesty or Theft
_____ Physical Limitation/Disability
_____ Overstayed Leave of Absence
_____ Retirement
_____ Death
_____ Reduction in Work Force
_____ Misconduct
_____ Disruptive Influence on Work Force
_____ Other (Explain)_____

Reason for Leaving (Supervisor or Department Head's Statement)

_____
_____

EMPLOYE EVALUATION (By Supervisor)

	Excellent	Good	Fair	Poor
Quality of Work				
Quantity of Work				
Conduct				
Attendance				
Overall Rating				

If allowed by local plant policy, would you re-employ in your department? _____ Yes _____ No

If not, why? Remarks _____
_____

Signature: _____
(Supervisor)

Reason for Leaving (Employe's Statement) _____
_____
_____
_____
_____

Date: _____ _____   Signaure: _____
                                                              (Employe)

The signing of this document does not necessarily mean the signer is in agreement with its contents, but rather acknowledges the existence of the document.

**TERMINATION CHECKLIST FOR PERSONNEL DEPARTMENT USE ONLY

Personnel Department representative should check off each item when explained or secured.

EXPLAIN   SECURE FROM EMPLOYE

____Dental Insurance (expiration date_____)   ____New Address
____Hospital Insurance (expiration date_____)   ____New Telephone Number
____Life Insurance (expiration date _____)   ____Company Equipment (uniforms, tools, etc.)
____Retirement Policy   ____Accounting Department (cleared)
____Profit Sharing   ____Company Vehicle
____Severance Allowance   ____Permanent Advance (cleared)
____Vacation Hours Earned _____ : Accrued _____   ____Employe Identification Card
____Unemployment Benefits   ____Keys
____Savings Bonds (reimbursement)   ____A. D. T. Card
____DeSoto Stock Ownership   ____Lock and Locker
____Credit Union   ____MCI Computer Code Charged

	Number of Hours	Mail	Pick-Up	Received	Date
Pay Check					
Vacation Check					
Severance Allowance					
Scanlon Check					

CONVERSION PRIVILEGES FOR MEDICAL INSURANCE AND LIFE INSURANCE PLANS HAVE BEEN EXPLAINED AND CONVERSION FORMS HAVE BEEN RECEIVED.

Date:_____   Signature: _____
                                                            (Employe)

Interviewer's Comments: _____
_____
_____
_____
_____
_____

Date: _____   Signature: _____
                                                            (Interviewer)

Revised 5/85
       10/80
       10/76

3. Exit Interview

EMPLOYEE EXIT INTERVIEW		

EMPLOYEE NAME | **TERMINATION DATE** | **LENGTH OF SERVICE**

POSITION TITLE | **DIVISION/DEPARTMENT** | **IMMEDIATE SUPERVISOR**

STATEMENT: THE OPINIONS OF THE EMPLOYEE ARE VERY IMPORTANT IN ASSISTING THE CORPORATION IN EVALUATING CURRENT PERSONNEL POLICIES AND EMPLOYMENT CONDITIONS. AS A PART OF YOUR TERMINATION, WE SOLICIT YOUR COOPERATION IN MEETING THIS OBJECTIVE, AND ASK THAT YOU VOLUNTARILY COMPLETE THE FOLLOWING QUESTIONNAIRE:

I. REASON(S) FOR LEAVING

II. IF REASON FOR LEAVING IS "NEW POSITION", PLEASE COMPLETE SECTION BELOW.

NAME OF COMPANY OR ORGANIZATION	LOCATION (City, State)	POSITION TITLE

III. GENERAL IMPRESSIONS OF YOUR SPECIFIC DEPARTMENT/DIVISION.

IMMEDIATE SUPERVISOR	
WORKING CONDITIONS	
WORK ASSIGNMENTS	
ADVANCEMENT OPPORTUNITIES	
OTHERS	

IV. GENERAL IMPRESSIONS OF THE CORPORATION

SALARIES & SALARY ADMIN	
WORKING CONDITIONS	
BENEFITS	
MANAGEMENT	
OTHERS	

V. WOULD YOU EVER DESIRE TO RETURN TO COMSAT? IF YES, UNDER WHAT CONDITIONS.

EMPLOYEE SIGNATURE	DATE

SPACE BELOW FOR PERSONNEL USE ONLY

INTERVIEWER'S COMMENTS

TYPE OF TERMINATION	INTERVIEWER	DATE
☐ VOLUNTARY ☐ INVOLUNTARY		

This is an official EEO compliance record

4. Exit Interview

Plant

EXIT INTERVIEW

Employee Name:_____ Job Title:_____

Dates of Employment: From_____ To_____ Length of Service_____

Department:_____ Foreman:_____

Have you been employed previously by Star:_____

Employee Benefits:
  Please indicate your thoughts on the following benefits.

Group Insurance:_____

Credit Union:_____

Retirement Plan:_____

Tuition Reimbursement:_____

Vacations/Holidays:_____

If we should make a change in our benefit program, what would you suggest?_____

_____

Do you feel that benefit information is well communicated to our employees?_____

_____

General Comments:_____

_____

Supervision & Training:

How do you feel about the adequacy and quality of the job training you received as
a new employee? _____

_____

Do you know the name of the leadman on your shift?_____

Did you attend an orientation session & an office tour within your 1st 6 weeks?____

Did you receive adequate supervision from your foreman?_____

_____

_____

Can you suggest improvements that might be made in the management of your department?

_____

_____

General Working Conditions:

Building & Grounds: _____

Equipment & Machines: _____

Parking Lot: _____

Lunchroom Facilities: _____

Safety: _____

Co-operation of Fellow Employees: _____

Others: _____

Do you feel that adequate safety measures are employed in the plant? _____
_____
_____

Do you have suggestions for improvements within your department? _____
_____
_____

Do you have suggestions that would benefit the entire company? _____
_____
_____

Your reasons for leaving Star: _____
_____
_____

If you have found other employment, what are the advantages of your new job over the position at Star? _____
_____
_____

For Industrial Relations Use Only:

Date: _____   Interviewer: _____

Comments: _____
_____

Date of Exit Feedback: _____

5. Exit Interview

EXIT INTERVIEW

EMPLOYEE'S NAME _____ EMP. NUMBER _____ SERVICE DATE _____ LAST DAY WORKED _____

JOB TITLE _____ DEPARTMENT _____ SUPERVISOR _____

I. WHY IS THIS EMPLOYEE LEAVING ▉▉▉▉▉▉▉▉▉▉?
    (IF DISCHARGE, GIVE EMPLOYEE'S PERCEPTION OF REASON):

II. WHAT FACTORS DID THE EMPLOYEE LIKE ABOUT WORKING HERE?

III. WHAT FACTORS WOULD THE EMPLOYEE LIKE TO SEE IMPROVED?

IV. COMMENTS OF THE EMPLOYEE ON HIS/HER SUPERVISION (INSTRUCTIONS, FAIRNESS, DEFINITION OF
    POLICIES, ANSWERING OF QUESTIONS, INTEREST IN EMPLOYEES AS PEOPLE):

V. WAS THE JOB FULLY DEFINED AND EXPLAINED?

VI. DID THE EMPLOYEE RECEIVE ADEQUATE TRAINING?

VII. COMMENTS OF EMPLOYEE ON ADVANCEMENT OPPORTUNITIES:

VIII. DEGREE OF SATISFACTION WITH: IX. (IF VOLUNTARY TERMINATION) WOULD THE
                                                EMPLOYEE CONSIDER WORKING HERE AGAIN IN
                                                THE FUTURE?

    A. INCOME:
    B. BENEFITS:
    C. WORKING CONDITIONS: ☐   YES   ☐   NO - WHY?
    D. CO-WORKER:

X. OTHER COMMENTS OR CONCERNS:

XI. REASON FOR TERMINATION:

☐ ANOTHER JOB, MORE PAY	☐ PERSONAL, ILLNESS	☐ OTHER DISCHARGE	
☐ ANOTHER JOB, DISSATISFIED	☐ PERSONAL, OTHER	☐ RETIREMENT	
☐ ANOTHER JOB, CAREER ADV.	☐ SCHOOL	OTHER:	
☐ ANOTHER JOB, OTHER	☐ LAYOFF		
☐ MILITARY SERVICE	☐ MEDICAL LAYOFF	☐ _____	
☐ SYSTEM TRANSFER	☐ PREGNANCY		
☐ PERSONAL, FAMILY MOVE	☐ MISCONDUCT-DISCHARGE	☐ _____	
☐ PERSONAL, FAMILY PROBLEMS	☐ ABSENCE DISCHARGE	☐ _____	
☐ PERSONAL, WORK PROBLEMS	☐ PROBATION DISCHARGE		

INTERVIEWER SIGNATURE _____ DATE _____

6. Exit Interview

Courtesy of *Rhonda Taghavi-Namin, Curtis Industries, Inc.*

CURTIS INDUSTRIES INC.

EXIT INTERVIEW

CODE: U = UNSATISFACTORY, F = FAIR,
S = SATISFACTORY, G = GOOD, E = EXCELLENT

PLEASE CHECK THE ONE
THAT MOST NEARLY APPLIES

U   F   S   G   E

1. GENERALLY SPEAKING, I WOULD RATE THIS COMPANY AS
   A _____ PLACE TO WORK.   ( ) ( ) ( ) ( ) ( )

2. WORKING CONDITIONS, RESTROOMS, AND PHYSICAL
   FACILITIES HERE ARE   ( ) ( ) ( ) ( ) ( )

3. MANAGEMENTS WILLINGNESS TO MAKE CORRECTIONS AND
   CHANGES IS   ( ) ( ) ( ) ( ) ( )

4. PAY LEVELS AT THIS COMPANY ARE GENERALLY   ( ) ( ) ( ) ( ) ( )

5. THE AMOUNT OF TRAINING I RECEIVED WHEN I FIRST
   CAME HERE WAS   ( ) ( ) ( ) ( ) ( )

6. MY UNDERSTANDING OF THE DUTIES AND RESPONSIBILITIES
   OF MY JOB IS   ( ) ( ) ( ) ( ) ( )

7. MY UNDERSTANDING OF WHAT PERFORMANCE STANDARDS
   I AM EXPECTED TO MEET IS   ( ) ( ) ( ) ( ) ( )

8. WHEN I DO A JOB WELL, THE RECOGNITION I RECEIVE IS   ( ) ( ) ( ) ( ) ( )

9. MY SUPERVISORS WILLINGNESS TO LISTEN TO MY PROBLEMS
   AND HELP ME WHEN I HAVE QUESTIONS IS   ( ) ( ) ( ) ( ) ( )

10. THE EXTENT TO WHICH I AM ENCOURAGED BY MY SUPERVISOR
    TO OFFER SUGGESTIONS AND IMPROVEMENTS IN WORK
    METHODS IS   ( ) ( ) ( ) ( ) ( )

11. DID YOU HAVE A PERFORMANCE REVIEW WITH YOUR
    SUPERVISOR AT LEAST ONCE A YEAR ? YES_____ NO_____

12. WHAT DID YOU LIKE MOST ABOUT WORKING HERE?_____
    _____

13. WHAT DID YOU LIKE LEAST ABOUT WORKING HERE?_____
    _____

14. WHAT ARE YOUR SUGGESTIONS FOR IMPROVING THIS COMPANY AS A PLACE TO WORK?_____
    _____
    _____
    _____

REASON FOR TERMINATION_____
_____

SIGNATURE_____ DATE_____

WITNESSED BY_____ DATE_____

60

7. Exit Interview

<u>Exit Interview</u>

Name:_____Department:_____

Last Day Worked:_____Termination Date:_____

Reason for Termination:___ _____

What are your plans for employment?_____

What influenced your decision to leave ▮▮▮▮▮▮?_____

Did you receive recognition from management?_____

Did management provide sufficient backing?_____

Was work challenging and rewarding?_____

Did you feel secure in your job?_____

Was there an opportunity to make personal contributions to the company?_____

_____

How did you like your job?_____

_____

Did you feel treated fairly by the company and your supervisor?_____

_____

Were working conditions, hours, equipment, fellow workers and facilities adequate?

_____

Were you properly instructed regarding your job duties?_____

How were the working conditions?_____

What did you think of your supervisor?_____

Did you think your rate of pay was fair?_____

What suggestions do you have that would help us improve   as a place to

work?_____

Additional Comments:_____

_____

Interviewed By:_____

Date:_____

8. Exit Interview

NAME_____ JOB TITLE_____

DEPARTMENT_____ SUPERVISOR_____

DATE EMPLOYED_____ DATE TERMINATED_____

1. Specific reasons for your leaving:_____

_____

2. How would you rate the general hospital orientation that you attended?

Very Good_____   Comments:_____
Good_____
Fair_____   _____
Poor_____

3. How would you rate your work area?

Attractive_____   Comments:_____
Moderately Attractive_____
Moderately Unattractive_____ _____
Unattractive_____

4. How would you rate the equipment you used in your work?

Very Good_____   Comments:_____
Good_____
Fair_____   _____
Poor_____

5. Do you feel that you have been treated with respect and courtesy by other employees?

Always_____   Comments:_____
Usually_____
Sometimes_____   _____
Never_____

6. How do you feel that your pay has compared with similar jobs in the community?

Higher_____   Comments:_____
About the Same_____
Lower_____   _____
Much Lower_____

7. How well do you think your department was run?

Very Effectively_____   Comments:_____
Effectively_____
Slightly ineffectively_____ _____
Very ineffectively_____

8. Did you feel free to discuss ideas and problems with your supervisor or Department Head?

Always_____   Comments:_____
Usually_____
Sometimes_____   _____
Never_____

9. Did your supervisor or Department Head give clear and definite instructions?

Yes_____   Comments:_____
No_____
                     _____

10. Did your supervisor or Department Head discuss your job performance with you?

Often_____   Comments:_____
Sufficiently_____
Very Seldom_____   _____
Never_____

11. Did you receive embarrassing criticism in the presence of fellow employees?

Never_____   Comments:_____
Occasionally_____
Often_____   _____

12. Has your supervisor or Department Head shown favoritism toward any of the workers under him/her?

Never_____   Comments:_____
Occasionally_____
Often_____   _____

13. Using the following scale, please rate our fringe benefits:

Very Good_____ (1)   Vacation_____
Moderately Good_____ (2)   Sick Leave_____
Good_____ (3)   Hospitalization_____
Moderately Poor_____ (4)   Life Insurance_____
Poor_____ (5)   Holidays_____
Very Poor_____ (6)   Disability_____
                                 Discounts_____
                                 Pension_____

14. How fairly are complaints handled?

Very Fairly_____   Comments:_____
Moderately fairly_____
Fairly_____   _____
Moderately Unfairly____
Unfairly_____
Very Unfairly_____

15. Would you recommend Wilson Memorial Hospital as a good place to work?

                            Comments:_____
Yes_____
No_____   _____

16. What suggestions do you have that would improve Wilson Memorial Hospital

_____

_____

_____

_____

17. Have you returned all hospital property?
Yes_____
No_____

18. Forwarding Address_____

_____

Interview Conducted by_____

Date:_____

9. Exit Interview

```
                         EXIT INTERVIEW


NAME _____   DATE OF EMPLOYMENT_____

ADDRESS_____   DATE OF TERMINATION_____

POSITION_____   DEPARTMENT_____

REASON FOR SEPARATION:_____

_____

1.  DID YOU LIKE WORKING FOR THE HOSPITAL?_____

2.  WHEN EMPLOYED, DID YOU FIND THE EMPLOYEES FRIENDLY AND CONGENIAL?_____

3.  IN YOUR OPINION, DID YOU HAVE A PROPER ORIENTATION?_____

4.  WERE THE EMPLOYEE BENEFIT PROGRAM AND PERSONNEL POLICIES EXPLAINED TO YOU?___

5.  DID YOUR SUPERVISOR EVALUATE YOUR PERFORMANCE?_____

6.  IN YOUR OPINION, WHAT DO YOU THINK IS THE WEAKNESS IN THE DEPARTMENT WHERE YOU WORKED?

    _____

    _____

7.  WHAT WERE THE STRONG POINTS IN THE DEPARTMENT?_____

    _____

8.  DO YOU FEEL THAT YOU WERE ALWAYS TREATED FAIRLY?  IF NOT, EXPLAIN, PLEASE?__

    _____

    _____

9.  WOULD YOU RECOMMEND YOUR FRIENDS TO WORK HERE?_____

10. WHAT SUGGESTIONS COULD YOU OFFER TO MAKE THIS A BETTER PLACE TO WORK?_____

    _____

    _____

    _____

    COMMENTS:_____

    _____

    _____

    _____

    _____

    THANK YOU FOR YOUR CO-OPERATION.
```

10. Exit Interview

EXIT INTERVIEW FORM

TO BE COMPLETED BY EMPLOYEE

NAME			SOC. SEC. NO.	DATE
ADDRESS			TEL. NO.	DATE OF HIRE

CLASSIFICATION	SALARY	DEPT. AND DISTRICT	SUPERVISOR

REASON FOR LEAVING

_____

_____

_____

EMPLOYEE'S COMMENTS

_____

_____

_____

_____

_____

_____

_____

_____ EMPLOYEE'S SIGNATURE

INTERVIEWER'S COMMENTS

_____

_____

_____

_____

_____

_____ INTERVIEWER'S SIGNATURE

65

11. Exit Interview

<u>Exit Interview</u>

Plant _____ Date_____

Name_____Department_____Supervisor_____

Date Employed_____Date Terminated_____Job_____

Do you have another job?_____Where_____

Did you voluntarily quit?_____Were you discharged?_____

Give reasons:_____

_____

_____

Were you Satisfied: or   Dissatisfied with:

___( )_____( )_____Advancement Opportunities?

___( )_____( )_____Your Rate of Pay?

___( )_____( )_____Shift Assignments?

___( )_____( )_____Working Conditions?

___( )_____( )_____Your Supervisor?

___( )_____( )_____Job Training?

___( )_____( )_____Fellow Employees?

___( )_____( )_____Fringe Benefits?

___( )_____( )_____Other Reasons?

COMMENTS:_____

_____

_____

Do you have any questions concerning the effect of this termination on any benefits you

may have?_____Subjects questioned:_____Disposition:_____

Reviewed By:_____Signed:_____
                 Superintendent   Employee

_____Interviewed by:_____
                                                                          Personnel Director

_____

Personnel Department follow-up:_____

_____

EP   374

13. Exit Questionnaire

Courtesy of *United Health Care*

℗ℙ

Physicians Health Plan
OF MINNESOTA

A HEALTH MAINTENANCE ORGANIZATION

NAME _____

DATE _____   EXIT QUESTIONNAIRE

1. HOW WOULD YOU RATE YOUR SUPERVISOR ON THE FOLLOWING POINTS?

	Almost Always	Usually	Sometimes	Never
a. Treats all employees equally	_____	_____	_____	_____
b. Well informed on how well you perform your job	_____	_____	_____	_____
c. Is readily accessible to employees for consultation	_____	_____	_____	_____
d. Resolves complaints, grievances and problems	_____	_____	_____	_____
e. Develops cooperation	_____	_____	_____	_____
f. Recognizes good work	_____	_____	_____	_____

2. IN YOUR DEPARTMENT, HOW WOULD YOU RATE THE FOLLOWING?

	Excellent	Good	Fair	Poor
a. Cooperation within Dept.	_____	_____	_____	_____
b. Cooperation with other Depts.	_____	_____	_____	_____
c. Physical setting	_____	_____	_____	_____

3. HOW WOULD YOU RATE COMMUNICATIONS WITH YOUR DEPARTMENT?

_____ Excellent   _____ Good   _____ Fair   _____ Poor

What makes you feel this way?

4. HOW WOULD YOU RATE COMMUNICATIONS WITH YOUR DEPARTMENT?

_____ Very Helpful   _____ Helpful

_____ Slightly Helpful   _____ Not Helpful

What could have improved the training?

-OVER-

500 OPUS CENTER · 9900 BREN ROAD EAST · MINNETONKA MINNESOTA 55343 · (612) 936 1200

5. WHAT DID YOU LIKE BEST ABOUT WORK AT PHYSICIANS HEALTH PLAN?

6. WHAT DID YOU LIKE LEAST?

7. WAS TRANSPORTATION TO WORK CONVENIENT FOR YOU?

    ( ) Yes   ( ) No

8. WHY ARE YOU LEAVING YOUR EMPLOYMENT WITH PHP?

14. Exit Questionnaire

EXIT QUESTIONNAIRE

Name (Optional) _____

Department _____

Length of Employment _____

Position Held _____

-Job Satisfaction:
____ A. Genuinely happy with your job
____ B. Job was acceptable
____ C. Dissatisfied with job

Comments:_____
_____
_____

-Working Conditions:
____ A. Pleasant environment
____ B. Generally acceptable
____ C. Poor

Comments:_____
_____
_____

-Communication:
____ A. Departmental personnel made genuine effort to keep staff informed
____ B. Received most information, but not always timely
____ C. Hardly ever got information, had to seek it out

Comments:_____
_____
_____

-Promotional Opportunities:
____ A. Felt many opportunities existed
____ B. Felt there are some opportunities
____ C. Feel opportunities were non-existent

Comments:_____
_____
_____

-Salary:
____ A. Good--better than most in comparable positions
____ B. Average
____ C. Poor--less than others in comparable positions

Comments:_____
_____
_____

-Fringe Benefits:
____ A. Good--better than most in the area
____ B. Average--comparable to others in area
____ C. Poor--not as good as others

Comments:_____
_____
_____

-Supervisor's Role:
____ A. Felt supervisor was instrumental in establishing a positive work environment
____ B. Supervisor's role was generally more positive than negative
____ C. Supervisor's influence was definitely detrimental to morale

Comments:_____
_____
_____

-Supervision:
____ A. Felt supervisor gave necessary guidance and information to operate efficiently
____ B. Guidance generally given, but sometimes had to teach yourself
____ C. Guidance seldom given, even when needed

Comments:_____
_____
_____

-Job's Challenge:
_____ A. Found job challenging
_____ B. Sometimes bored
_____ C. Job was routine and boring

Comments: _____
_____
_____

-Recognition:
_____ A. Felt supervisor was aware of
           your work and gave recogni-
           tion for achievement and
           extra effort
_____ B. Supervisor sometimes acknow-
           ledged extra effort
_____ C. Supervisor generally failed
           to acknowledge performance

Comments: _____
_____
_____

-Workload:
_____ A. Found workload to be chal-
           lenging but fair
_____ B. Didn't have enough to do
_____ C. Continually had more work
           than you could complete

Comments: _____
_____
_____

-Working Relationships:
_____ A. Other staff helpful and har-
           monious working conditions
           existed
_____ B. Staff generally got along
_____ C. Little cooperation among
_____   staff

Comments: _____
_____
_____

List the reasons why you are leaving
(in order of importance):

1. _____
   _____

2. _____
   _____

3. _____
   _____

4. _____
   _____

5. _____
   _____

Other Comments: _____
_____
_____
_____
_____
_____
_____
_____
_____
_____
_____
_____
_____

15. Post Employment Survey
Courtesy of *FBG Service Corporation*

F.B.G. SERVICE CORPORATION
DES MOINES, IOWA

POST EMPLOYMENT SURVEY

ORIENTATION

1. Did you feel sufficiently trained for your work? Yes___ No___

   If no, explain_____

   _____

   _____

2. Did you feel informed about your work? Yes___ No___

3. Where you explained all your job duties before starting work? Yes___ No___

   If no, explain_____

   _____

SUPERVISION

1. How did you get along with your supervisor?_____

2. Did your supervisor present you with instructions about your work that was easily understood? Yes___ No___

3. Did you feel your were treated fairly by your supervisor? Yes___ No___

   If no, explain_____

   _____

3. Were any problems you may have had with your job and its duties fully explained to you? Yes___ No___

   If no, explain_____

   _____

4. Where you given ample time to make any corrections in your job performance that was brought to your attention? Yes__ No__

   If no, explain_____

   _____

ATTITUDE TOWARD F.B.G. SERVICE CORPORATION

1. How did you feel about your rate of pay?_____

2. What did you think about FBG as a place to work?_____

   _____

(over)

71

3. Would you want to return to FBG in the future? Yes___ No___

4. Reason for your termination_____
   Termination date_____

Comments: (please use this space for any additional items you want to
          bring to our attention)

_____

_____

_____

_____

_____

_____

                              _____   _____
                               Employee Signature   Date

16. Notice of Resignation

NOTICE OF RESIGNATION

From: _____

To: _____
                    (Dept. Head or Supervisor)

I wish to resign from my position as _____

effective on _____ My last day of work will be _____

Reason or reasons for this action are as follows: _____

_____

_____

_____

FROM: _____ DEPARTMENT: _____

TO: Personnel Office

	EXCELLENT	GOOD	FAIR	POOR*
Quality of work performed	( )	( )	( )	( )
Quantity of work performed	( )	( )	( )	( )
Attendance/punctuality	( )	( )	( )	( )
Adherence to hospital and department policies	( )	( )	( )	( )
Contribution to positive work climate and team effort	( )	( )	( )	( )
Ability to work with minimum supervision	( )	( )	( )	( )

*rating in this column must be fully justified in writing.

I would ( ) / would not ( ) reemploy this individual.

REMARKS: _____

_____

_____

I do ( ) /do not ( ) authorize the personnel office to release my references to future employers.

_____   _____
(Signature of Employee)   (Date)

DATE: _____ SIGNATURE: _____
                                          (Department Head or Supervisor)

17. Letter of Resignation

Courtesy of FBG Service Corporation

FBG SERVICE CORPORATION
605 - 17th Street
Des Moines, Iowa 50309

Date: _____

Subject: Letter of Resignation

To: _____

1. I, _____ do hereby tender my resignation to FBG Service Corporation. My last day of work will be _____.

2. I am submitting my resignation for the following reason(s):

   ____ Another Job   ____ Home Responsibilities   ____ Retirement
   ____ Death in Family   ____ Illness in Family   ____ Returning to School
   ____ Dissatisfaction with Job ____ Leaving the City   ____ Seek other Employment
   ____ Getting Married   ____ Lost means of Transportation ____ Working Conditions
   ____ Health   ____ Pregnancy

   ____ Other (Please Explain) _____

3. Additional Comments: _____

   _____

   _____

4. My Forwarding Address will be: _____

   _____

   _____

   _____
   Employee's Signature

   _____
   Job Title

   _____
   Department

5. Supervisor's Remarks: _____

   _____

   _____   _____
   Signature - Supervisor   Date

   _____   _____
   Signature - Office   Date

18. Resignation Statement

_____ CORPORATION
_____

RESIGNATION STATEMENT

(To Be Completed and Forwarded to Personnel Immediately Upon Notification)

EMPLOYEE'S NAME _____ DATE _____

TITLE _____ LOCATION _____ DEPT. _____

I am voluntarily resigning my employment at ███████. as of _____
                                                                    DATE

My reasons for leaving are as follows:_____
_____
_____
_____
_____
_____

I have discussed my resignation with my supervisor and agree that my resignation is
voluntary on my part.

I am _____ am not _____ leaving my present position to accept other work with
another company.

(Please indicate name of company if accepting another position)._____
_____

I am _____ am not _____ interested in a transfer.

I would _____ would not _____ be interested in Re-employment.

_____
Signature of Employee   Date
_____

SUPERVISOR COMMENTS _____
_____
_____

Eligible for rehire   Yes _____   No _____

_____ _____ _____
          Signature   Title   Date

_____
Copy to: Employee __   Personnel Office __   Manager/Supervisor __

19. Resignation Form

RESIGNATION

NAME_____ DATE_____

EMPLOYEE NO._____ TIME_____

I HEREBY SUBMIT MY RESIGNATION TO ████████████████████████████

EFFECTIVE_____.

I WISH TO MAKE CLEAR THAT I HAVE NO CLAIMS, OR GROUNDS FOR ANY CLAIMS

AGAINST MY EMPLOYER BASED ON MY TIME OF EMPLOYMENT WITH THE COMPANY.

MY REASON FOR LEAVING_____

_____
EMPLOYER'S ACCEPTANCE

_____
EMPLOYEE SIGNATURE

MANAGEMENT SUMMARY

A FORM RECOMMENDED FOR USE DURING THE EXIT INTERVIEW DESIGNED TO RELEASE THE EMPLOYER FROM JUDGMENTAL DECISIONS ON FUTURE REFERENCE CHECKS.

INFORMATION RELEASE FOR REFERENCE CHECKS

This agreement allows my former employer to release the following information to prospective employers, if such information is required.

Annual Earnings

Hourly Rate/Salary

Dates of employment

Recorded (Documented) Discipline

Recorded (Documented) Commendations

Positison(s) Held

Home Address During Employment

General Comments as Recorded on Preformance Evaluations

Reason for Leaving Company

Eligibility for Rehire

I have personally authorized _____to release information on _____specific areas only. I understand no
       No. of boxes checked
information will be released unless a request is made by telephone or in writing by a prospective employer. I will hold my former employer harmless for authorized information released.

_____
Signed   Date

_____
Witness   Date

21. Employee Separation

Your Company

Employee Separation

Date: _____

Employee: _____   Employee Number: _____

Department: _____   Last Day of Work: _____

Job Title: _____

Reason for Resignation: _____

Forwarding Address: _____

Each terminating employee is requested to complete a confidential Exit Interview with a representative of the Personnel Department. Please schedule this interview with your supervisor, and note the date and time below:

_____
Employee's Signature

Exit Interview: Time: _____

Date: _____

_____
Supervisor

TO BE COMPLETED BY SUPERVISOR:

SEPARATED: ☐ Resignation   ☐ Discharge   ☐ Other (Explain)_____

Reason for Separation _____

Termination Effective Date _____   Last Day Worked _____

If these two dates vary, please explain _____

Notice Given?   ☐ Yes   ☐ No   Date _____   Eligible for Rehire?   ☐ Yes   ☐ No

If Not, Explain Fully _____

PERSONNEL OFFICE USE ONLY: PDO: ☐ Paid ☐ Unpaid   Number of additional hours to be paid_____

Explanation if additional
hours are to be paid   _____

CANCELLATIONS: BC/BS ☐   L.I. ☐   I.N.A. ☐   Termination Code: |__|__| PDO
Accrual |·|__|__|__|__|__|
DEDUCTION CODE: |__|__| |__|__| |__|__|
|__|__|
|__|__|

AUTHORIZATION

Department Head _____

Personnel _____

Payroll _____

PE-05

22. Termination Report
Courtesy of *On-Line Software International, Inc.*

TERMINATION REPORT

Last Name _____ First _____ Middle Initial _____

Department _____ Effective Date of Termination _____

Type of Separation (Check One)

- □ Resignation (attach letter of resignation)   □ Dismissal
- □ Mutual Agreement   □ Other _____
- □ Layoff

Reason for Separation:
- □ Absenteeism/Lateness   □ Changing Job   □ Family
- □ Health   □ Incompetence   □ Reduction in Force
- □ Other: _____

Employee Evaluation

Recommendation:
- □ Without Reservation
- □ With Some Reservation
- □ Would Not Recommend

Rehire? □ Yes □ No

	Unsatisfactory	Fair	Satisfactory	Good	Excellent
Attendance					
Cooperation					
Initiative					
Job Knowledge					
Quality of Work					

Final Accounting

Severance: _____   Vacation pay (days): _____

Insurance Coverage: _____   Other (1) _____ $ _____

(1 month max. for layoff)   (2) _____ $ _____

                                                     (3) _____ $ _____

Special Pay Instructions _____

_____

Additional Comments: _____

_____

Department Head Signature: _____ Date: _____

Please complete a "Request for Personnel" form if this position is to be refilled.

For Personnel Use

- □ Memo to distribution
- □ Conversion letter with form
- □ Adjust floor plan
- □ Move file with notation
- □ Delete on premium stmt.
- □ Move Home Life enrollment card to historical section
- □ Advise accounting

- □ Access card
- □ Keys (master, office, car)
- □ Home Life ID card
- □ PCS card
- □ Les Elites card
- □ AVIS card
- □ Take off all lists
- □ Terminate PCS coverage

- □ Note on calendars
- □ Advise librarian
- □ Advise Data Center
- □ For involuntary terminations, fill out "Instructions for claiming unemployment benefits"

Original - Personnel   Copy - Accounting

23. Departure Processing

Your Company

DEPARTURE PROCESSING

_____   _____
Name   Last Day Worked

Please have all items listed below initialed by the proper person indicated. This completed form must be returned to the Personnel Department/Director's Office before you receive your final check.

Items To Be Returned	Return Items To
____ return employee ID card	Director's Office/Personnel
____ return all lab coats	Supervisor, Linen Supply
____ return all library books/periodicals	Medical Librarian
____ settle all pharmacy charges	General Accounting Clerk
____ return all hospital supplies and equipment	Supervisor or Department Head
____ return all hospital keys	Supervisor or Department Head
____ return pocket page unit	Director's Office/Engineering

FINAL CHECK DISTRIBUTION

Please complete the following in regard to your final check:

____ My check is currently direct-deposited. Please mail the check stub to the address given below.

____ Please mail my final check to the following address:

_____

_____

_____

____ I will come by the Personnel Department/Director's Office to pick up my final check.

_____   _____
Personnel Department/Director's Office   Date Received

24. Involuntary Termination Review

Your Company

CONFIDENTIAL

INVOLUNTARY TERMINATION REVIEW

Concerning: _____ Date of Hire _____ Date of Termination _____

Title: _____ Location _____ Department _____

Name of Person Preparing this Review _____ Date of this Review _____

It is ▉▉▉▉ policy to carefully record the factors involved in each involuntary termination. This important document *supplements* the Personnel Action Notice; it does not replace it, nor is it replaced by it. In the space below (attach additional page(s) if necessary), explain in detail:

A.   The reason(s) why the employee was released. You are to be very specific and must include all factors involved in this termination.

_____
_____
_____
_____
_____

B.   History of warning/advisement concerning deficiencies/other factors.

_____
_____
_____
_____

C.   What you told the employee at time of release. (It is recognized that discretion/judgment sometimes dictate giving an employee an explanation other than the specific factors explained under item A, above.)

_____
_____
_____
_____
_____

D.   Employee reaction to the involuntary termination.

_____
_____
_____
_____

E.   Other relevant information concerning this involuntary termination.

_____
_____
_____
_____
_____

25. Employee Termination Routing Form

Personnel File   <u>EMPLOYEE TERMINATION ROUTING FORM</u>   Date _____

1) PERSONNEL MGR

     A)   Gets person's current address, etc. and where he/she can be reached or mail forwarded

         NAME _____

         1)   Add. _____

         2)   Phone # _____

     B)   Indicates if any monies due _____

     C)   If a resignation, gets it in writing.

     D)   Notes termination date. _____

     E)   Takes name off Staff List and adds to monthly Personnel report.

     F)   Adjusts Insurance plan.

     G)   Hands employee Insurance conversion information.

     H)   Makes note to issue memo that employee is leaving, and who designated replacement is.

     I)   Sends Termination Form to supervisor to fill out.

     J)   Sends person to senior.

                                         _____
                                             Signature

2) _____
   Senior

     A)   Collects all manuals, notebooks, drawings, notes, reports, documents, or any other property belonging to
     B)   Receives status report of work in progress.
     C)   If desired by senior, has person put together or update hat.

                      hat = Job Manual _____
                                               Signature

3) VP _____

     A)   Ensures all job related matters are handled.

                                         _____
                                               Signature

Rev.23Jan85

4) FACILITIES MGR

   A) Makes sure all personal material is removed.
   B) Makes sure post area is clean.
   C) Gets keys.

   _____
   Signature

5) MIS DIR

   A) Handles computer access as needed.

   _____
   Signature

6) DISB MGR

   A) Determines any monies due (refer to step "B" under
      Personnel Manager). _____.
   B) Determines if any more is forthcoming. Y/N. If yes, what
   _____.
   C) Notes that employee is terminating and files pay folder in Finance
      Archives.
   D) Verifies that current address is on file.

   _____
   Signature

7) TRAINING DIR

   A) Receives staff and Job Manuals.
   B) Removes from training log book.
   C) Sends student folder to Archives.
   D) Changes Org Board accordingly.

   _____
   Signature

8) PERS MGR

   A) Files graphs in personnel file.
   B) Has employee sign Termination Statement.
   C) Ensures all steps on routing form have been done.
   D) Notes any information needed for future reference.
   E) Shows individual out
   F) Files this routing form along with contract and Termination Statement
      in Personnel file.
   G) Files Personnel file in Ex-staff files.

   _____
   Signature

END

IHF:D2#6

Rev.23Jan85

83

26. Termination Check-off List

TERMINATION CHECK-OFF LIST

NAME_____

DEPARTMENT_____

TERMINATION DATE_____

REASON FOR TERMINATION*_____

_____

/___/   PROBATION REPORT IN EMPLOYEE PORTFOLIO

/___/   RESIGNATION

/___/   TERMINATION NOTIFICATION

/___/   NOTIFY PAYROLL

/___/   NOTIFY LOAN DEPARTMENT

/___/   CONVERSION/CONTINUATION LETTER

/___/   CANCEL MEDICAL INSURANCE

/___/   CANCEL LIFE INSURANCE

/___/   REMOVE FROM ███ SECURITY SYSTEM

/___/   REMOVE ████████ HOME DIRECTORY

/___/   REMOVE FROM DEPARTMENTAL PERSONNEL INFORMATION

/___/   CHANGE TIME CARD

/___/   ADD TO EMPLOYEE TERMINATIONS LISTING

/___/   REMOVE FROM PERSONNEL BIRTHDAY LISTING

/___/   REMOVE FROM ██████ SERVICE PINS LISTING

/___/   CLOSE EMPLOYEE PORTFOLIO

27. Termination Statement

<u>Termination Statement</u>

I hereby certify that I do not have in my possession, nor have I failed to return, any notebooks, drawings, notes, reports, proposals, or other documents or materials (or copies or extracts thereof) or tools, equipment, or other property belonging to

I also certify that I have complied with and will continue to comply with all of the provisions of the Agreement regarding proprietary information which I have previously signed, including my obligation to preserve as confidential all proprietary, technical, and business information pertaining to

All monies due me have been received by me.

I have been advised of my Medical/Dental and Life insurance benefit conversion privilege, and of the date in which my benefits will no longer be available to me through the Group Plan. I have not suffered from any Worker's Compensation injury or illness while at

By:_____   _____
        Signature   Date

Witness:_____   _____
              Authorized Signature   Date

IHF:D6#31